The Willie Lynch Letter
&
The Making Of A Slave

Published By:

Lushena Books
607 Country Club Drive, Unit E
Bensenville, IL 60106

Tel: 630-238-8708
Fax: 630-238-8824
Email: Lushenabks@yahoo.com

Distributed By Lushena Books
607 Country club Drive, Unit E
Bensenville, IL 60106
Tel: 630-238-8708
Fax: 630-238-8824

Historical Documentary
Layout & Cover Graphic Design
by Kashif Malik Hassan-EL

Published February, 1999
Second Printing August, 1999

INTRODUCTION

The infamous **"Willie Lynch"** letter gives both African and Caucasian students and teachers some insight, concerning the brutal and inhumane psychology behind the African slave trade. The materialistic viewpoint of Southern plantation owners that slavery was a **"business"** and the victims of chattel slavery were merely pawns in an economic game of debauchery, cross-breeding, inter-racial rape and mental conditioning of a negroid race, they considered sub-human.

Equally important is the international nature of the European economic, political and cultural climate, that influenced the slave trade. Within the time scale of African History, it was a relatively short period, a mere one and a half centuries -- from the most intensive phase of the Atlantic slave trade to the advent of European administration and dominance. Long before that the Slave coast had been chartered by the Portuguese and the people off the area west of Benin, between the Volta River and Lagos, European traders traced a cultural history which linked them with the earliest Yoruba settlements to the north and eastern borders of Africa.[1]

There were considerable debates during the colonial periods in the United States, and the late 1700's, the attention of the national government was mainly directed to slavery and the rising numbers of slaves traded and imported into the South.

The first debate was held in Congress, in 1789, on the question of whether taxes should be paid on imported slaves.

During the debate on the slavery duty bill, which was introduced by Mr. Clymer's committee, Parker of Virginia moved that on May 13, 1789 a tax of ten dollars per capita be laid on slaves imported.[2] He plainly stated that the tax was designed to check the trade, and that he was sorry that the Constitution prevented Congress from prohibiting the importation altogether. The proposal was evidently unwelcome and caused extended debate. Smith of South Carolina wanted to postpone the matter " so big with the serious consequences to the State he represented ".

Roger Sherman of Connecticut "could not reconcile himself to the insertion of human beings as an article of duty, among goods, wares, and merchandise". Jackson of Georgia argued against any restriction, and thought such states as Virginia " ought to let their neighbors get supplied, before they imposed such a burden upon the importation ".

Some Congressmen argued during that Congress " should wipe off the stigma under which America laboured ". This brought Jackson again to his feet. He believed, in spite of the fashion of the day," that Negroes were better off as slaves than as freedmen, and that, as the tax was partial, it would be the most odious tax Congress could impose ".

Such sentiments were a distinct advance in pro-slavery doctrine, and called for a protest from Congressman Madison of Virginia.

There were both moral arguments and legal positions to the questions of slavery in the South. On one side, it began with the "*Rights of Man* ", and descended to stickling for it to have a decent appearance on the statute-book.

On the other side, it began with the uplifting of the heathen; and descended to a denial of the applicability of moral principles to the question; said Holland of North Carolina: " It is admitted that the condition of slaves in the Southern states is much superior to that of those in Africa ". (Holland's opinion) Who, then, will say that trade is immoral? But , in fact, morality has nothing to with this traffic, for Joseph Clay declared, " it must appear to every man of common sense, that the question could be considered in a commercial point of view only ".[2]

The other side declared that, " by laws of God and man these captured Negroes, are entitled to their freedom as clearly and as absolutely as we are." Nevertheless, some were willing to leave them to the tender mercies of the Slaves states, so long as the statue-book was not disgraced by no explicit recognition of slavery.

The moral questions were argued back and forth, but there were no question of the tremendous profitability using slavery in exchange for molasses, sugar, textiles, spices, and the massive free labour of cotton production on numerous plantations in the South. The system began with a conspiratorial battle of wits between the European traders and African chiefs. Slave traders were required to know not only the state of the trade, if they were to " see a profit ", but also to know the likely supply of the slaves available on one hand, and the likely supply of ships on the other.

Also the varying values of many different standards of payment. Coins were seldom or never used on the coast. Mostly the chiefs and slave traders dealt in rolls of tobacco, barrels of rum, and firearms and generally in lengths of iron or copper, or in pots and basins of brass. The slaver's books are full of all of this.[3]

Regardless of the economic prosperity enjoyed during the African slave trade, and the tedious burden placed on the backs of African people, most will agree the psychological damage, and atrocities inflicted on Black people during that point of time, and even today, are the most outrageous examples of injustice and downpression ever experienced by humanity.

February, 1999

Kashif Malik Hassan-EL

Bibliography

1). The Western Slave Coast and It's Rulers
-- Newbury

2.) The Suppression of the African Slave Trade to the United States of America: 1638-1870
-- W.E.B. DuBois

3.) The African Slave Trade, Pre-Colonial History 1450-1850
-- Basil Davidson

WILLIAM LYNCH

THE UNTOLD "STORY" 1712

This speech was delivered by a white slave owner, William Lynch on the bank of the James River in 1712.

And The Message is Still True... TODAY

By William Lynch

Gentlemen, I greet you here on the banks of the James River in the year of our Lord one thousand seven hundred and twelve. First, I shall thank you , the gentlemen of the Colony of Virginia for bringing me here . I am here to help you solve some of your problems with slaves. Your invitation reached me on my modest plantation in the West Indies where I have experimented with some of the newest and still the oldest methods for control of slaves. Ancient Rome would envy us if my program is implemented. As our boat sailed south on the James River, named for our Illustrious King, whose version of the Bible we cherish. I saw enough to know that your problem is not unique. While Rome used cords of wood as crosses for standing human bodies along it's old highways in great numbers, you are here using the tree and the rope on occasion.

I caught the whiff of a dead slave hanging from a tree a couple of miles back. You are not only losing valuable stock by hangings, you are having uprisings, slaves are running away, your crops are sometimes left in the fields too long for maximum profit, you suffer occasional fires, your animals are killed. Gentlemen, you know what your problems are; I do not need to elaborate. I am not here to enumerate your problems; however, I am here to introduce you to method of solving them.

In my bag here, ***I have a foolproof method for controlling your Black slaves.*** I guarantee every one of you that if installed correctly, ***it will control the slaves for at least 300 hundred years.*** My method is simple. Any member of your family or your overseer can use it.

I have outlined a number of DIFFERENCES among the slaves, and I take these differences and make them bigger. I use FEAR, DISTRUST, and ENVY for control purposes. These methods have worked on my modest plantation in the West Indies and it will work throughout the South. Take this simple little list of differences, and think about them. On top of my list is ***"AGE" but it is there only because it starts with an "A"; the second is "COLOR" or SHADE, there is INTELLIGENCE, SIZE, SEX, SIZE PLANTATIONS, STATUS ON PLANTATION, ATTITUDE OF OWNERS, WHETHER THE SLAVES LIVE IN THE VALLEY, ON THE HILL, EAST, WEST, NORTH, SOUTH, HAVE FINE HAIR, COURSE HAIR, OR IS TALL OR SHORT.*** Now that you have a list of differences, ***I shall give you an outline of action - but before that I shall assure you that DISTRUST is stronger than TRUST, and ENVY is stronger than ADULATION, RESPECT OR ADMIRATION.***

The Black slave after receiving this indoctrination shall carry on and will become self refueling and self generating for hundreds of years, maybe thousands.

Don,t forget **you must pitch the OLD BLACK MALE vs. THE YOUNG BLACK and the YOUNG BLACK MALE against the OLD BLACK MALE. You must use the Dark Skin Slaves vs. the Light Skin Slaves and the Light Skin Slaves vs. the Dark Skin Slaves. You must use the Female vs. the Male, and the Male vs. the Female. You must also have your white servants and overseers Distrust all Blacks, but it is necessary that your slaves trust and depend on us . They must love, respect and trust only us.**

Gentlemen, these kits are your keys to control. Use them. Have your wives and children use them, never miss an opportunity. If used intensively for one year, the slaves themselves will remain perpetually distrustful. Thank you, gentlemen.

Editor's repeat: This speech was delivered by a white slave owner, William Lynch, on the banks of the James River in 1712.

LET'S MAKE A SLAVE
by

The Black Arcade Liberation Library

1970

It was the interest and business of slave holders to study human nature, and the slave nature in particular, with a view to practical results, and many of them attained astonishing proficiently in this direction. They had to deal not with earth, wood, and stone, but with men, and they by every regard they had for their safety and prosperity they had need to know the material on which they were to work. Conscious of the injustice and wrong they were every hour perpetrating and knowing what they themselves would do were they the victims of such wrongs, they were constantly looking for the first signs of the dread retribution. They watched, therefore, with skilled and practiced eyes, and learned to read, with great accuracy, the state of mind and heart of the slave, through his sable face. Unusual sobriety, apparent abstraction, sullenness, and indifference--indeed, any mood out of the common way afforded ground for suspicion and inquiry.

Frederick Douglas

LET'S MAKE A SLAVE is a study of the scientific process of man breaking and slave making. It describes the rationale and results of the Anglo Saxon's ideas and methods of insuring the master/slave relationship.

Travelling sailors disseminated news, rumor, and style among far-flung black people, contributing to the creation of a shared African identity and multiple black identities. Above is two Africans contesting in a head-butting contest as drawn in Venezuela. Sailors from the eastern seaboard of North America frequently mingled with the local people, and completed in African-inspired martial arts contests.

LET'S MAKE A SLAVE

The Origin and Development of a Social Being
Called the Negro

Let us make a slave a slave. What do I need? First of all we need a black nigger man, a pregnant nigger woman and her baby nigger boy. Second, I will use the same basic principle that we use in the breaking a horse, combined with some more sustaining factors.

When we do it with horses we break them from one form of life to another; that is, we reduce them from their natural state in nature; whereas nature provides them with the natural capacity to take of their needs and the needs of their offspring, we break that natural string of independence from them and thereby create a dependency state so that we may be able to get from them useful production for our business and pleasure.

CARDINAL PRINCIPLES FOR MAKING A NEGRO

For fear that our future generations may not understand the principles of breaking both horses and man, we lay down the art. For, if we are to sustain our basic economy we must break and tie both of the beasts together, the nigger and the horse. We understand that short range planning in economics results in periodic economic chaos; so that, to avoid turmoil in the economy, it requires us to have breath and depth in long range comprehensive planning, articulating both skills and sharp perception.

We lay down the following principles for long range comprehensive economic planning:

1.) Both horse and nigger are no good to the economy in the wild or natural state.
2.) Both must be broken and tied together for orderly production.
3.) For the orderly futures, special and particular attention must be paid to the female and the young offspring.
4.) Both must be crossbred to produce a variety and division of labor.
5.) Both must be taught to respond to a particular new language.
6.) Psychological and physical instruction of containment must be created for both.

We hold the above six cardinal principles as trues to be self-evident, based on the following discourse concerning the economics of breaking and tying the horse and the nigger together -- all inclusive of the six principles laid down above.

NOTE: Neither principles alone will suffice for good economics. All principles must be employed for the orderly good of the nation.

Accordingly, both a wild horse and a wild or natural nigger is dangerous even if captured for they will have a tendency to seek their customary freedom, and, in doing so, might kill you in your sleep. You cannot rest. They sleep while you are awake and are awake while you asleep. They are dangerous near the family house and it requires too much labor to watch them away from the house. Above all you cannot get them to work in the natural state. Hence, both the horse and the nigger must be broken that is break them from one form of mental life to another-- keep the body and take the mind. In other words, break the will to resist. Now the breaking process is the same for both the horse and nigger, only slightly varying in degrees. But as we said before, there is an art in long range economic planning. You must keep your eye and thoughts on the female and the offspring of the horse and the nigger.

A brief discourse in offspring development will shed light on the key to sound economic principles. Pay little attention to the generation of original breaking but concentrate on future generations. Therefore, if you break the female mother, she will break the offspring in its early years of development and, when the offspring is old enough to work, she will deliver it up to you for her normal female protective tendencies will have been lost in the original breaking process.

For example, take the case of the wild stud horse, a female horse and an already infant horse and compare the breaking process with two captured nigger males in their natural state, a pregnant nigger woman with her infant offspring. Take the stud horse, break him for limited containment. Completely break the female horse until she becomes very gentle whereas you or anybody can ride her in comfort. Breed the mare and the stud until you have the desired offspring. Then you can turn the stud to freedom until you need him again. Train the female horse whereby she will eat out of your hand, and she will in turn train the infant horse to eat out of your hand also.

When it comes to breaking the uncivilized nigger, use the same process, but vary the degree and step up the pressure so as to do a complete reversal of the mind. Take the meanest and most restless nigger, strip him of his clothes in front of the remaining male niggers, the female, and the nigger infant, tar and feather him, tie each leg to a different horse in opposite directions, set him a fire and beat both horses to pull him apart in front of the remaining niggers. The next step is to take a bullwhip and beat the remaining nigger male to the point of death in front of the female and the infant. Don't kill him, but ***put the fear of God in him, for he can be useful for future breeding.***

THE BREAKING PROCESS OF THE AFRICAN WOMAN

Then take the female run a series of tests on her to see if she will submit to your desires willingly. Test her in every way because she is the most important factor for good economics. If she shows any sign of resistance in submitting completely to your will, do not hesitate to use the bull whip on her to extract the last bit of bitch out of her. Take care not to kill her, for, in doing so, you spoil good economics. When in complete submission, she will train her offspring in the early years to submit to labor when they become of age.

Understanding is the best thing. Therefore, we shall go deeper into this area of the subject matter concerning what we have produced here in this breaking process of the female nigger. We have reversed the relationships. In her natural uncivilized state she would have a strong dependency on the uncivilized nigger male, and she would have a limited protective tendency toward her independent male offspring and would raise the female offspring to be dependent like her. Nature had provided for this type of balance. ***We reversed nature by burning and pulling one civilized nigger apart and bull whipping the other to the point of death -- all in her presence.*** By her being left alone, unprotected, with the male image destroyed, the ordeal caused her to move from her psychological dependent state to a frozen independent state. **In this frozen psychological state of**

independence she will raise her male and female offspring in reversed roles. For fear of the young male's life, she will psychologically train him to be mentally weak and dependent but physically strong.
Because she has become psychologically independent, she will train her female offspring's to be psychologically independent. ***What have you got?*** **You've got the nigger woman out front and the man behind and scared. This is a perfect situation for sound sleep and economics.**

Before the breaking process, we had to be alertly on guard at all times. Now we can sleep soundly, for out of Frozen fear, his woman stands guard for us. He cannot get past her infant slave process. ***HE IS A GOOD TOOL, NOW READY TO BE TIED TO THE HORSE AT A TENDER AGE.***

By the time a nigger boy reaches the age of sixteen, he is soundly broken in and ready for life's sound and efficient work and the reproduction of a unit of good labor force.

Continually, though the breaking of uncivilized savage niggers, by throwing the nigger female savage into a frozen psychological state of independency, by killing of the protective male image by creating a submissive dependent mind of the nigger male savage, we have created an orbiting cycle that turns in its own axis forever, unless a phenomenon occurs and reshifts the positions of the female savages. We show what we mean by example. Take the case of the two economic slave units and examine them closely.

" I been drug and put through the shackles so bad I done forgot some of my children's names." Laura Clarke, age 87, near Livingston, Sumter County, Alabama. Born in North Carolina and brought to Alabama as a child.

THE NEGRO MARRIAGE UNIT:

We breed two nigger males with two nigger females. Then we take the nigger males from them and keep them moving and working. Say the one nigger female bear a nigger female and the other bears a nigger male. Both nigger females, being without the influence of the nigger image, frozen with an independent psychology, will raise their offspring into reverse positions. The one with the female offspring will teach her to be like herself, independent and negotiable (**we negotiate with her, through her, by her and negotiate her at will**). The one with the nigger male offspring, she being frozen with a subconscious fear for his life, will raise him to be mentally dependent and weak, but physically strong-- in other words, body over mind. Now in a few years when these two offsprings become fertile for early reproduction, we will mate and breed them and continue the cycle. That is good, sound, and long range comprehensive planning.

WARNING: POSSIBLE INTERLOPING NEGATIVES

Earlier, we talked about the non-economic good of the horses and the nigger in their wild or natural state: We talked out the principle of breaking and tying them together for orderly production. Furthermore, we talked about paying particular attention to the female savage and her offspring orderly future planning; then, more recently we stated that, by reversing the positions of the male and the female savages, we had created an orbiting cycle that turns on its own axis forever, until this phenomenon occurred and reshifted the positions of the male and female savages.

Our experts warned us about the possibility of this phenomenon occurring, for they say the mind has a strong drive to correct and recorrect itself over a period of time. If it can touch substantial original historical base; and they advised us that the best way to deal with the phenomenon is to shave off the brute's mental history and create a multiplicity of phenomena of illusions that each illusion will twirl in it's own orbit, something similar to floating balls in a vacuum.

This creation of a multiplicity of phenomena of illusions entails the principles of cross-breeding the nigger and the horse as we stated above, the purpose of which is to create a diversified division of labor thereby creating different levels of labor and different values of illusions at each connecting level of labor, the results of which is the severance of the points of original beginnings for each sphere illusion.

Since we feel that the subject matter may get more complicated as we proceed in laying down our economic plan concerning the purpose, reasons, and effect of cross-breeding horses and niggers, we shall lay down the following definitional terms for future generations:

1.) Orbiting cycle means a thing turning in a given path.

2.) Axis means upon which or around which a body turns.

3.) Phenomenon means something beyond ordinary conception and inspires awe and wonder.

4.) Multiplicity means a great number.

5.) Sphere means a globe.

6.) Cross-breeding a horse means taking a horse and breeding it with an ass longheaded mule that is not reproductive nor productive by itself.

7.) Cross-breeding niggers means taking as many drops of good white blood and putting them into as many nigger women as possible, varying the drops by various tones that you want, and then letting them breed with each other until circle of colors appear as you desire. What this means is this: Put the niggers and the horse in the breeding pot, mix some asses and some good white blood and what do you get?

You got a multiplicity of colors of ass backward, unusual niggers, running, tied to backward ass long-headed mules, the productive of itself, the other sterile *(THE ONE CONSTANT, THE OTHER DYING-- WE KEEP THE NIGGER CONSTANT FOR WE MAY REPLACE THE MULE FOR ANOTHER TOOL, BOTH MULE AND NIGGER TIED TO EACH OTHER, NEITHER KNOWING WHERE THE OTHER CAME FROM AND NEITHER PRODUCTIVE FOR ITSELF, NOR WITHOUT EACH OTHER.)*

CONTROLLED LANGUAGE

Cross-breeding completed, for further severance from their original beginning, ***we must completely annihilate the mother tongue*** to both the new nigger and the new mule and institute a new language that involves the new life's work of both. You know language is a peculiar institution. It leads to the heart of a people. The more a foreigner knows about the language of another country the more he is able to move through all levels of that society. Therefore, if the foreigner is an enemy of another country, to the extent that he knows the body of the language, to that extent is the country vulnerable to attack or invasion of a foreign culture. For example, you take a slave, if you teach him all about your language, he will know all your secrets, and he is then no more a slave, for you can't fool him any longer, and ***being a fool is one of the basic ingredients of and incidents to the maintenance of the slavery system.***

For example if you told a slave that he must perform in getting out *"OUR CROPS"* and he knows the language well, he would know that *"OUR CROPS"* didn't mean *"OUR" CROPS*, and the slavery system would break down, for he would relate on the basis of what *"OUR CROPS"* really meant.

So you have to be careful in setting up the new language for the slave would soon be in your house, talking to you as *"MAN TO MAN"* and that is death to our economic system.

In addition, the definition of words or terms is only a minute part of the process. Values are created and transported by communication through the body of the language. A total society has many interconnected value systems. All these values in the society have bridges of language to connect them for orderly working in the society, but for these language bridges, these many value systems would shapely clash and cause internal strife or civil war, the degree of the conflict being determined by the magnitude of issues or relative opposing strength in whatever form. For example, if you put a slave in a hog pen and train him to life there and incorporate in him to value it as a way of life completely, the biggest problem you would have out of him is that he would worry you about provisions to keep the hog pen clean, or partially clean, or he might not worry you at all. On the other hand, if you put this same slave in the same hog pen and make a slip and incorporate something in his language whereby he comes to value a house more than he does his hog pen, you got a problem. He will soon be in your house.

" My mammy was a fine weaver; this is her spinning wheel." Lucindy Lawrence Jurdon, age 79, Lee County, Alabama. Born 1858, Macon County, Georgia. Slave in Georgia.

FOOD FOR THOUGHT FROM THE INTERNET

Dear Black Americans:

After all of these years and all we have been through together, we think it's appropriate for us to show our gratitude for all you have done for us.

We have chastised you, criticized you, punished you, and in some cases even apologized to you, but we have never formally nor publicly thanked you for your never-ending allegiance and support to our cause.

This is our open letter of thanks. We will always be in your debt to you for your labor. You built this country and were responsible for the great wealth we still enjoy today. Upon your backs, laden with the stripes we sometimes had to apply for disciplinary reasons, you carried our nation.

We thank you for your diligence and your tenacity. Even when we refused to allow you to even walk in our shadows, you followed close behind believing that someday we would accept you and treat you like men and women.

We publicly acknowledge Black people for raising our children, attending to our sick, and preparing our meals while we were occupied with the trappings of the good life.

Even during the time when we found pleasure in your women and enjoyment in seeing your men lynched, maimed and burned, some of you continued to watch over us and our belongings.

We simply cannot thank you enough.

Your bravery on the battlefield, despite being classified as three-fifths of a man, was and still is outstanding. We often watched in awe as you went about your prescribed chores and assignments, sometimes laboring in the hot sun for 12 hours, to assist in realizing our dreams of wealth and good fortune.

Now that we control at least 90 percent of all of the resources and wealth of this nation, we have Black people to thank the most. We can only think of the sacrifices you and your families made to make it all possible.

You were there when it all began, and you are still with us today, protecting us from those Black people who have the temerity to speak out against our past transgressions.

Thank you for continuing to bring 95 percent of what you earn to our businesses.

Thanks for buying our **Hilfigers, Karans, Nikes**, and all the other brands you so adore.

Your super-rich athletes, entertainers, intellectuals, and business persons (both legal and illegal) exchange most of their money for our cars, jewelry, homes, and clothing. What a windfall they have provided for us!

The less fortunate among you spend all they have at our neighborhood stores, enabling us to open even more stores. Sure, they complain about us, but they never do anything to hurt us economically.

Allow us to thank you for not bogging yourself down with the business of doing business with your own people. We can take care of that for you.

You just keep doing business with us. It's safer that way. Besides, everything you need, we make anyway, even Kente cloth. You just continue to dance, sing and distrust and hate one another.

"Thank you for not doing business with your own people. We can take care of that for you."

Have yourself a good time, and this time we'll take of you. It's the least we can do, considering all you've done for us. Heck you deserve it, Black people. For all your labor, which created our wealth, for your resisting the messages of trouble making Blacks like Washington, Delany, Garvey, Bethune, Tubman, and Truth, for fighting and dying on our battlefields, we thank you.

And we really thank you for not reading about the many Black warriors that participated in the development of our great country. We thank you for keeping it hidden from the younger generation. Thank you for not bringing such glorious deeds to our attention.

For allowing us to move into your neighborhoods, we will forever be grateful to you. For your unceasing desire to be near us and for hardly ever following through on your threats due to our lack of reciprocity and equity -- we thank you so much.

We also appreciate your acquiescence to our political agendas, for abdicating your own economic self-sufficiency, and for working so diligently for the economic well-being of our people. You are real troopers.

And, even though the 13th, 14th, and 15th Amendments were written for you and many of your relatives died for the rights described therein, you did not resist when we changed those Black rights to civil rights and allowed virtually every other group to take advantage of them as well.

Black people, you are something else! Your dependence upon us to do the right thing is beyond our imagination, irrespective of what we do to you and the many promises we have made and broken. But, this time we will make it right, we promise. Trust us.

Tell you what. You don't need your own hotels. You can continue to stay in ours. You have no need for supermarkets when you can shop at ours 24 hours a day. Why should you even think about owning more banks? You have plenty now. And don't waste your energies trying to break into manufacturing.
You worked hard enough in our fields.

Relax. Have a party. We'll sell you everything you need. And when you die, we'll even bury you at a discount. How's that for gratitude?

Finally, the best part. You went beyond the pale and turned over your children to us for their education. With what we have taught them, it's likely they will continue in a mode similar to the one you have followed for the past 45 years (since school desegregation).

When Mr. Lynch walked on the banks of the James River in 1712 and said he would make us a slave for 300 years, little did he realize the truth of his prediction. Just 13 more years and his promise will come to fruition. But with two generation of your children having gone through our education systems, we can look forward to at least another 50 years of prosperity. Things could not be better -- it's all because of you. For all you have done, we thank you from the bottom of our hearts, *Black Americans*. You're the best friends any group of people could ever have!

Sincerely,

All Other Americans

Few Americans, black or white, recognize the degree to which early African American history is a maritime history. W. Jeffrey Bolster shatters the myth that the black seafaring in the age of sail was limited to the Middle Passage. Seafaring was one of the most significant occupations among both enslaved and free black men between 1790 and 1865. Ten of thousands of black seamen sailed on lofty clippers and modest coasters. They sailed in whalers, warships and privateers. Some were slaves, forced to work at sea, but by 1800 most were free man, seeking liberation and economic opportunity aboard ship.

Black Jacks places sailors of color squarely at the center of the Atlantic maritime culture. W. Jeffrey Bolster deserves our thanks for recovering an exciting, essential chapter in African-American history, one that not only deepens our appreciation for the roles black men played (as both able seaman and buccaneers, but also vividly demonstrates the fluidity and multi-dimensional complexity of black identity."

--CHARLES JOHNSON,
AUTHOR OF "MIDDLE PASSAGE"

Lushena Books would like to thank W. Jeffrey Bolster, for his excellent book on Black American sailors, which shows an important , but often neglected aspect of American History. And for the use of pictures and written material, which were included within this book.